UP HERE

A COMFORTING BOOK FOR FAMILIES OF CHILDREN IN HEAVEN

Written and Illustrated by

KATIE SWANSON

Enchanted Bonding
BOOKS
est 2024

EnchantedBondingBooks.com

IN LOVING MEMORY OF

Now is your time of grief, but I will
see you again and you will rejoice,
and no one will take away your joy.
John 16:22

Dedicated to

all of the babies gone too soon.

The babies born sleeping.
Those we carried but never held.
Those we held but could not take home.
Those we brought home but could not stay.

They are forever in our hearts and will never be forgotten.

And to my perfect baby boy,
Sawyer Swanson
August 10-11, 2023

In my grief for you, I acknowledge that your body is no
longer here, but you are still alive in everything that I do.
I know that if love could have saved you,
you would have lived forever.

Until we are together again,

Mama

Up here, the sun always shines and the birds always sing. Up here is an angelic eternal spring.

There is no day and there is no night. There is no darkness, only light.

What do you think Heaven looks like?

Up here, I have everything
that I could ever want or need.
Whenever I'd like to,
I sit down to read.

I never lack things to do. I am never bored.
I even get to talk with the Lord.

What do you think _____ does in Heaven?

Up here, I can hear your wishes and dreams.
Your passions and talents simply beam.

I am proud when you accomplish
the things you set your mind to.
You can do anything when you see it through.

What are some of your talents?

Up here, I can feel your love
coming from your heart. It makes me
feel like we aren't so far apart.

Whenever you feel sad, I see your crying soul,
but let my love for you make you feel whole.

What are some things that make you feel better when you're sad?

Up here, we have parties and celebrations!
We gather together with all generations.

When you have a birthday, I sing to you.
Can you hear it?
You cannot see me, but I'm there in spirit.

Up here, God tells me the secrets of the universe.
He shares his knowledge from the beginning
of time up to my birth.

He knows what has happened and what will happen next.
I try to understand, but it's very complex.

What do you think God's purpose for you is?

Up here, I want you to know that I am safe,
so I leave signs to show you that I care.
Perhaps I painted that rainbow or
sent that butterfly to land in your hair.

What are some things that remind you of _____?

Up here, I play with other kids on a playground
bigger than you can imagine.
We run and jump and laugh with such passion.

Some of the children have siblings like me and
others left just their parents to grieve.
We all know that you miss us, but please keep in
mind that we had to leave Earth,
it was just our time.

*How do you think you can help
mommy/daddy feel better during this tough time?*

Up here, I dance to the sound of harps.
The angels compliment me and make kind remarks.
I create a gentile gust when I twirl.
I make the autumn breeze sway and swirl.

Up here, our family members cuddle me and tell me stories of you.
I learn about your day and how much you grew.

They never want to put me down, they pass me all around.
I'm safe and cozy in their arms. Their love for me's profound.

And all the pets we've ever owned leap across the
Rainbow Bridge to say, "Hey! Welcome home!"

Up here, the angels sing me lullabies.
Their voices are pure like the clear blue sky.

When you lie in bed at night and listen really close,
maybe you can hear the angels singing songs
that you love most.

What songs do you think the angels sing to ______?

Up here, I am never sad or mad, I only ever feel
glad. I smile from ear to ear and don't ever feel fear.

I know that you're sad that I am not with you, but
my purpose on Earth is something only God knew.
My purpose is done. I know it's hard to believe it,
but be proud of me that I have achieved it.

I am safe and I am happy.
I never feel pain and joyful I will remain.

Up here, I wait for you, but time moves differently here.
A million days on Earth is not even a year.

One day when you're old and grown, with gray hair and have
lived a life you adore, it will be your time to join me
and we will be together just like before.

What would you like to say to ______ when you see him/her in Heaven?

Up here is Heaven and Heaven is where
I'm meant to be.

Don't feel sad for me, because
I'm eternally free.

A LETTER FROM

If you purchased or were gifted this book, then I want to offer my condolences for your loss. I know all too well what your family is experiencing. After two miscarriages, I then lost my healthy and beautiful, newborn son, Sawyer just 17 hours after he was born. He passed away from an umbilical cord entanglement. What we have in common is that we were inducted into this club that we never wanted to be a part of. We are families of baby loss. I want to offer some words that will hopefully bring you a bit of peace during this impossible time.

After my baby boy died in my arms just hours after I had birthed him, I struggled with my faith. I was angry at God. I did not understand how he could bless us with such a perfect baby just to take him away immediately. I fell into a whirlwind of depression, rage, and jealousy. But as time moved on, I started noticing that my son was still very much alive in my heart and soul. In fact, he is the reason that you are holding this book in your hands right now.

THE AUTHOR

It's impossible to believe that our baby died for no reason. Every soul is placed on this Earth for a purpose. God does not "waste" lives. Some people don't fulfill their purpose until they have spent 100 years here. Other souls, like our precious babies, completed God's purpose in their short time here. Think of all the ways that your child made an impact on your life - big or small. In my case, Sawyer's existence helped me find new friendships and weed out the ones that should have been many years ago. He helped my husband and I become closer than ever. Sawyer inspired me to become an author and advocate for baby loss awareness and support.

Maybe your child helped you learn to live a healthier lifestyle? Or maybe their existence and subsequent loss inspired you to change your career to something that you're more passionate about? Walking my own journey of loss, I recognize that some beautiful flowers have begun to grow in the shadows of Sawyer's absence. As the years go on, we will continue to discover how our child's life impacted this world.

It does not make losing our children any easier, but it personally makes me so profoundly proud to be a mother of a child in Heaven. He could accomplish what he was put on Earth to do in just ten months while some souls take decades. Your child is just as unique and special as mine is. They are home with the Lord and they never have to endure heartache, anger, envy, or pain. They only ever knew love and will feel nothing but love for all of eternity in the arms of Jesus. We will see them again in Heaven and it will become clear to us why they had to leave us so soon. I am proud of your child. I am proud of you.

"YOU DO NOT UNDERSTAND WHAT I AM DOING NOW, BUT SOMEDAY, YOU WILL."
JOHN 13:7

WITH GRATITUDE AND COMPASSION,
KATIE SWANSON